The *Green* Bubbie

Ruth Pinkenson Feldman EdD

Dedication

In beloved memory of my mother, Anne Warnick Pinkenson, A"H,
and in honor of my children, my grandchildren, and all my "sprouts"

The midrashic author, Rabbi Yehuda the son of Rabbi Seemon, quotes a verse from Deuteronomy (13:5) that tells us to "...walk after God..."—to emulate Him. But, says Rabbi Yehuda, we know that walking after God is impossible, because we cannot follow His paths in the sea or ascend to the sky and cleave to His fiery Divine presence. How, then, can we emulate Him? Rabbi Yehuda's answer is simple: "From the beginning of the creation of the world, the Holy One blessed be He engaged first in planting, as it is written, *And God the Lord planted a garden in Eden...* (Genesis 2:8).

Introduction

There is something about life that is better when shared. Green Bubbie is the new name for a treasured relationship that we warm to when we are very young and never outgrow. Even if we don't have biological relatives, we can all have, or become, a Green Bubbie. We all need role models, and a healthy dose of unconditional love, acceptance, and the occasional big hug!

The Green Bubbie is a new, energy-efficient model of grand parenting. You don't even have to have your own kids—you can nurture somebody else's sprouts!

The Green Bubbie shares lessons from the garden as metaphors to help cultivate a new image of a woman of any age who thrives in relationships, appreciates her heritage, and recognizes that she has plenty to learn and plenty to share.

Recently I was walking through the local playground when I encountered a young mother with her two-year-old son. Rebecca had been a high school classmate of my own daughter. When I bent down to speak directly to her son, Rebecca explained that he didn't like to talk. So I asked him if he would like to come and dig in my garden. He nodded. I asked if he would need a big shovel as he looked quite strong. He said yes. I nodded and suggested that he visit the garden some day soon. A few weeks later I got an e-mail from Rebecca. She sent a transcript of an actual conversation she had had with her son. He began by asking, "Where's Mr. Feldman?" After a few attempts to figure out what he was talking about, she said to him, "Oh, you mean *Mrs.* Feldman. She is probably in her house." To which he responded, "No, she's in her garden."

Now let's revisit this. For sure, I made a new friend with the two-year-old who remembered the garden invitation. But his mom found a kindred spirit in the form of a Green Bubbie with whom she could share the story. People want to share their lives, and we all want people to be interested in our children. There is plenty of attention floating around that could be directed to real people, to connect them. In one small gesture we created a three-generation link of interest, and a Green Bubbie planted the seed of friendship.

A Green Bubbie relationship is noncommercial and mindful. It is in the moment, it is a spontaneous acknowledgement and connection between generations. It does not need to be long term and it has nothing to do with money. You can't hire a Green Bubbie.

In addition to being a Green Bubbie, I am also an artist, a gardener, a mother, a grandmother, a wife, a friend, and a lifelong learner. I learn about life: in the garden, in the home, and in community. As a Jewish woman, I learn Torah and classical works of Jewish wisdom. For twelve years I was the Director of Early Childhood Education for the Jewish Community Centers Association of North America. I traveled across the continent and met tens of thousands of parents, teachers, and young children. While teaching Jewish values from Jewish texts, I witnessed firsthand the transformational power of traditional Jewish wisdom to bolster families and to empower parents to teach their children what Judaism offers as a road map for how to live in this world.

I began to think about what else I could do with my energy and my passion for living and loving. I knew that I was very inspired by nature, and I knew how important and rewarding it was to teach Jewish values to young children. So, Torah and the Natural World. As I began to think of the idea, I thought I'd create a persona, the Green Bubbie(™))—a Jewish, female Mr. Rogers, if you will, who would be kind and talk to children about how the world works. Then, when I began to talk about the idea, I realized that adults in general want to talk about how the world works and what the Torah has to say about life. Everybody had her own idea of what a Green Bubbie could be!

In the past few years I have been blessed to see my children marry, have their own children, and become strong stakeholders in the Jewish communities where they live. Our family is very close, but we live far apart. I can't tell you when it happened, but at some point my husband and I became "established pillars" in our own community—which sounds like we've been turned into stone! NOT SO! But we have become living pillars to scaffold the new shoots—the "sprouts" that are growing all around us.

My husband and I attended several Shabbat retreats at Kayam Farm, at The Pearlstone Retreat Center in Reisterstown, Maryland, and met wonderful groups of young Jews exploring Torah as they plowed their way into sustainable agricultural endeavors. Together with the Jewish Farm School, they were planning their next 3-day Beit Midrash, a retreat to study Jewish texts dealing with the Torah's laws of agriculture. They asked me to be the co-chair, along with an undergraduate college student. These weren't my children, but they were the age of my children, and many of them were happy to have someone to call "Green Bubbie."

So I have spent the last few years doing "field work" as the Green Bubbie. And in the process, I have learned that there is a yearning for intergenerational connection, there is a desire to learn the roots of Jewish wisdom, and there is a new concept of what it is to be, and to have, a Bubbie.

I am writing this book to share with you the tremendous joy and the potential *nachas*—a special kind of Jewish pride—that you can reap from connecting with others, and with other people's children, as well as your own.

I am certainly not the only Green Bubbie; you too can be one, or you may already be one and just don't know it. Try it on: Green Bubbies come in all sizes. If you have been blessed to know your tradition and you have been the recipient of unconditional love, become a Green Bubbie. Be a role model of a wonderful life that is still blooming.

Look around you—there may be sprouts growing right in front of you. Branch out, get connected, nourish others, and feel yourself thrive!

Table of Contents

One

Why a *Green* Bubbie?

"Each generation will praise Your works to the next generation and retell Your mighty deeds..." Psalm 145:4.

Why *"Green?"*

*G*reen is life. When you cut a branch from a tree, if it is still green, it is alive. So too with all of us: if we are "green" we are growing, breathing, flexible, and, if we are wise, still learning.

Becoming a Green Bubbie is about renewal, not recycling. Although, as you take this path, you will learn that you have far more to recycle than just empty bottles and cans.

"The righteous will flourish like a palm tree, tall as the Cedars of Lebanon, planted in the House of the Lord, blossoming in His courtyards. They will still bear fruit in old age, they will stay vigorous and fresh." (Psalm 92).   So there you have it: a Biblical source for the Green Bubbie! *She is righteous, vigorous, and still blooming!*

And why a "Bubbie"?

"Bubbie" is an endearing Yiddish name for grandmother. But a "green bubbie" is not about being a biological grandmother. Green Bubbie is the name for a new organic relationship. A Green Bubbie grafts generations together. While it is a new name, we are all familiar with the concepts of role models, community building, and being a link in the chain of tradition. A Green Bubbie is a different kind of mentor—she is a spiritual guide to the next stage of the life you're now living. Think of her as the accidental relative you happen to discover on the road to finding yourself.

The tradition a Green Bubbie is transmitting is the Torah of lovingkindness, love, and of being family. A Green Bubbie is connecting with others through spiritual DNA. This is not about bequeathing your jewelry or paying anyone's tuition. There is no financial component.

Having a Green Bubbie puts you into a caring, loving relationship. It gives you an opportunity to call someone "Bubbie," one of the most endearing of names, and to experience a dose of unconditional love. Giving someone permission to call you Bubbie acknowledges a special relationship. It is a level of respect that says, "Yes, I know there is an age and generational distance between us, but I would like to be connected, related to you in some special way."

This book is not about aging—it is about living. This is *not* a self-help book. This is not about self-healing—it is about self-sharing. There are a few stages in life when you get to try on a new identity; perhaps the first nickname your friends give you, or when you're first called Doctor, or Mom, or Auntie. And now, here comes another opportunity for a new identity. As a Green Bubbie, you take a new path, one that you can help chart yourself.

You don't have to be Jewish to be or to have a Green Bubbie. However, the Jewish tradition is the root of my life—it is what I am and what I share. And my garden grows in the Mid-Atlantic region of the United States, the planting zone from which I draw my experiences and the metaphors that I will share with you.

Why are Green Bubbies needed now?

Life's journey is taking an increasingly circuitous route. When we look around, many of us are far from the home in which we were raised. You may be traveling to countries whose names your parents can't pronounce, or your grandchildren may be raising grains that you only thought of as stock futures. You may be more or less religious than your parents. You may be geographically removed from your native land. You may be speaking in a computer language, or tweeting to thousands of friends in a nano-second across the globe. "Green Bubbie" is a new name for an old way of relating to each other: generation to generation, person to person, in real time, with direct eye contact!

As more women have postponed marriage and childbearing, the distance between generations has increased. Grandparents became older, and families moved farther and farther apart. So much has changed in this new millennium, but nothing has changed more than the nature and definition of family. It seems that everything that was most fundamental about child bearing, child rearing, family formation, and forming identity is now open for discussion.

But one area still seems to be intact, and that is generational succession. You still can't get old before you're young! A Green Bubbie has the wisdom that comes from a life well lived. A generational link is a precious gift and, until now, it has been the primary mode of transmission for family, culture, community, and religion. And it isn't just content that grandparents can transmit—it is the experience of acceptance, the feeling that someone is interested in what is going on inside of you, regardless of what your outside looks like.

Finding someone a few years ahead of you can provide a generational comfort zone. Meeting someone who shares the values, world view, and language of the community you now call your own can be a source of support, direction, and connection. Judaism used to be a one-way transmission from one generation to the next. This is one of the first generations of young women that has had the benefit of widespread learning of Jewish wisdom directly from Jewish texts. So you may find that you and your sprouts are coming with different modes of Jewish learning, but nevertheless you have much to offer each other.

Green Bubbie's Spirituality

Being a Green Bubbie is an opportunity to be a power source for your own spiritual/emotional ecosystem. It doesn't matter how many degrees you have or how accomplished you are; when you continue to learn, when you maintain within you a zest for new experiences and horizons, you keep yourself current and make the longitudinal pathway more inviting.

"Ben Zoma used to say, 'Who is wise? The person who learns from everyone.'" Pirkei Avot 4:1. A Green Bubbie is wise. She learns from everyone, and that is what everyone can learn from her.

In the late 1960s, the conventional wisdom warned young women of the limitations of being defined only as someone's wife, mother, daughter, or even sister. The point of our identity search was to have an independent identity, a life of one's own, apart from family. Well, no matter how accomplished I am and regardless of my professional identity, I love being in relationships—lots of them! Being a Green Bubbie is a way of cultivating even more.

The challenge for women of my generation was "having it all." I have more than enough. The Green Bubbie is not about having it all—it is about *giving* your all. You don't give yourself away, but what you do give, you give with a full heart.

This "becoming a Green Bubbie" is about abundance, the recognition of the myriad blessings you have received and your insatiable desire to share what you know. Judaism is all about relationships, interpersonal ones, with ourselves, intergenerational relationships, and with God.

Life is a journey, and sometimes we don't even know where we are headed until we meet someone, and say to ourselves, "I'd like my life to be like that." Just as you can't develop emotional intelligence from reading about it in books, so, too, spiritual development is learned with people and from people. It is about recognizing lives marked by lovingkindness, respect, and holiness.

Judaism teaches that we are all created in the image of God—*b'tzelem Elokim, Imago Dei*—it is what interconnects us to each other; it is what we have in common, and our purpose in life is to be more like God. And what does God expect from us? As it says in Deuteronomy, "To walk in His ways, to do justice, and to love peace." Our task is to figure out how to walk in God's ways.

What are God's attributes that we can emulate? "God is ... compassionate and gracious, slow to anger, and abundant in kindness and truth." Exodus 34:6. It is the attribute of compassion, *rachamim* that I believe is the most accessible and essential for a Green Bubbie. The root of the Hebrew word *rachamim* is *rechem;* it means "womb," the quintessentially female aspect.

Each of us is created in the image of God, and born from a womb of a mother. Like the love of a mother, *rachamim,* the attribute of God's loving compassion is the basis of how we can relate to one another. What an incredible source to draw from, what a magnificent goal toward which to strive.

The Green Bubbie also learns from the garden. In the Torah's account of Creation, God created the natural world before creating people. That is a pretty powerful lesson in humility. The "garden" was here before us, and it will be here long after we are gone. A Green Bubbie asks, "What can I learn from the plants? From the earth? From the natural world? And, what can I leave for others?"

Get in touch with your inner source of compassion, your *rachamim;* unlock your reservoir of lovingkindness: Release your latent Green Bubbie power!

Two

Splitting Perennials

Hillel used to say, "If I am not for myself, who will be for me? If I am only for myself, what am I? And, If not now, when?" Pirkei Avot 1:14

*g*iving of yourself doesn't diminish you. Sharing yourself can strengthen you. When you give something of yourself, you create more space to spread out your roots and grow in new ways. As we learn from Hillel, there is a need for balance between the self and others. You can't think only of yourself, nor can you neglect yourself. If you don't take care of yourself, who else will? If you think only of yourself, the question becomes not "who" am I, but rather "what" am I? To think only of yourself removes you from the human condition, which is one of mutual responsibility and engagement. The final question, "If not now, when?" is not, in fact, a separate question; it refers to and is part of the first two. It is not sequential: first, I will take care of myself and then, I will think about others. No, it is a constant question–always striving for that balance, being present to the needs of others, as you are aware of your own self. It is not an abstract idea; it is the fundamental way for us to live together in this world.

A perennial garden is filled with flowers blooming at different times throughout the seasons. These same flowers reappear every year in the garden; there is no need to replant them. In fact, some may be "naturalizing," which means they spread themselves and increase in size and number over the years. While it is sometimes desirable to start flowers from seeds, it is also possible to start a garden by "splitting perennials." In this process, a mature planting can be subdivided—a part of its original root source gets "split" and replanted in another spot, and the original is free to grow fuller.

I'd like to tell you how I began to take lessons from the garden. After my mother died, a friend came to my home for the *Shiva* and brought primroses. Two small plants, each with dark green leaves and bright, colored flowers. And while they were beautiful, I remember saying to myself, "How odd; people usually bring food to a shiva house, flowers maybe, but plants?" On the other hand, I had never sat shiva before, so I was open to the idea that perhaps this was a tradition or custom I had just never heard of.

My mother died in the month of February, in the depth of winter. In the Hebrew calendar, it was the month of Adar, when the holiday of Purim is celebrated. Traditionally, the month of Adar is the happiest time of the year. The Talmud, says, "Whoever enters the month of Adar, *simcha* [joy] is magnified!" Well, trust me, there was no way I was able to magnify my joy. I was desolate, in deep despair and sadness. When the ground softened, I planted the primroses. The weeks passed and turned into months of crying, mourning, and longing, and then, at some point, the year of mourning my mother's death drew to a close. I was somewhat stunned that I noticed that the primroses were in bloom. I saw primroses everywhere I looked, in gardens, in the food co-op. I had never noticed primroses before.

My mourning period was ending, and I learned from the garden that a year had transpired, even as I learned from my first experience of commemorating the anniversary of my mother's death. A Yahrtzeit is how we mark the recurring date of death, just as birthdays mark the day of birth. For a Yahrtzeit, we light a candle and say the Kaddish prayer, and pray that our actions on this earth will elevate the soul of our loved one. For me, it was the beauty of the perennial flower reappearing in the garden that gave me faith in the cycle of life and showed me how to mark a year's duration in an otherwise endless process of mourning. The flower showed me that life continues, and we can look forward to the seasons of change, even as we mark and remember the death of loved ones. The annual cycle of blooming perennials marks the resurgence of life. From it we learn that growth happens without any of our controlling efforts.

One of my first Green Bubbies was a 70-something Christian woman named Harriet Heaney. Harriet knew the names of every one of her flowers, and the rows of her vegetables seemed endless and filled with magical vines and stories that connected each plant to its name and personality. The first plants she introduced me to were Bleeding Hearts, Pulmonary Vine, and Lung Wort. There was an immediacy and connection between what was growing in her garden and how we live, breath, and love as humans.

There was a kind of enchantment to her garden. As she introduced my very young children to her garden flower friends, she would bend down and touch them, almost shaking hands with Lady's Slipper and Jacob's Ladder. We felt like we knew them! I longed to write a children's book in which the flowers would speak to one another ("'Delphinium!' snapped the dragon!"). I remember saying to myself, "Someday I want to have a garden just like Harriet's, and I'll share it with other people's children, just as she is sharing hers with mine."

When I voiced my desire to begin gardening, Harriet immediately stuck her trowel into the base of her Bleeding Hearts (a spectacularly green plant with dangling pink heart-shaped flowers). "Start with this" she said, as she scooped out a small part of that plant, partial root and all. "Just dig a hole and plant this in the ground." And so I did.

As we continued to visit, we would enter through her garden's gate, which was left unlocked only at times when visitors were welcome. Harriet would fill empty flowerpots or buckets with a variety of clumps of flowering plants. When I would protest that she was giving me too much, she would say, "Don't worry, when you split the perennials, it's better for the plants, and the original one will grow even bigger."

And so I began to garden. The plants that could be divided from Harriet's garden became my garden, and when I moved to another neighborhood, I split those original plants and brought them to my new home. Harriet would come to visit bringing rhubarb from her garden, and I would return it to her in the form of strawberry-rhubarb pie. In other words, Harriet's garden continued to grow and live and thrive with me.

My lovely, generous friend shared more than her garden. Harriet did not have children of her own. She shared herself in a way that became a part of me, and that I can now share with others. She split her perennials with me, and I got a lot more than a garden of beautiful flowers. Now I am sharing my garden and myself with new generations of children, and turning their parents into gardeners, too.

Just like perennial flowers, we, too, can be subdivided to thrive in another garden — I'm not talking about human cloning here! When you see something in another person that you admire, observe that person, engage with her, and learn as much as you can from her. And if someone sees something in you, share yourself with her.

Consider yourself a perennial flowering plant, with a strong, although dividable, root base. Now, think of yourself as part of your family of origin, the one you were born into. What became of all of you? Did the family subdivide, with parents moving to the south or west? If there are siblings, did you choose the same paths? What do you share with them? When you think of your extended family—aunts, uncles, cousins—are you in touch with them? Do you consider yourself part of a clan? Do you have family reunions? I grew up thinking I had a huge extended family, but today, almost all of them are gone. Of those who are still alive, some chose not only different religious paths but different religions altogether and different geographic locales. A few, very few remain close.

My understanding of what is meant by "extended family" now goes way beyond my family of origin. In lieu of the classic family tree, we now have more of a rhizome—a knobby root that grows in many directions. I am part of a new, huge family—a community into which I have been replanted. I have taken root in the fertile soil created by people who are much more like the me I have become, and we are growing in the same direction.

My father, A"H, and then my mother-in-law, A"H, each lived the last years of their lives in our home. For more than six years we were a multigenerational household, but even then our branches grew out horizontally to others in our community, just as we were digging in to care for our parents. We never would have had the strength or the spiritual nutrients to care for them without our extended community pitching in and staking us up.

We need one another to raise healthy, thriving children, and we need one another to care for and nurture all generations in the community. We have more than one family: not only do we have a family of origin, we have the ones we create and the ones where we choose to live. I have lived in a number of different communities, and feel very blessed that all were nurturing, supportive, and filled with other transplants searching for their roots—both old and new—and finding fertile ground.

Each of the communities in which I have lived has been redivided and replanted, is continually involved in learning, and is growth-oriented. Regardless of their differences in observance, all in their own way shared our common Torah.

The Zohar teaches that "Israel, God, and Torah are one." I think a Green Bubbie shares this view. A Green Bubbie can demonstrate that no matter how many times the Jewish people subdivide themselves, just like a perennial flower, we have a common root system.

So much of Judaism happens within the family. And a Green Bubbie knows that no two families are the same. The Passover seder of your childhood may not be the one you have learned to share as an adult. If you find yourself alone, consider becoming the convener of a community seder—perhaps in your apartment building, your synagogue, or with your new friends from your art class. I am constantly astonished by how many people I never even thought were Jewish are delighted to be invited. Don't assume you are the only one without an invitation. And if you invite a family with young children, tell them they can put those "sprouts" to bed in your home, or encourage them to bring them in a stroller. Not everyone has grandchildren, and not every child has grandparents. Mix and match and nurture one another. Everyone has something to share and something to learn. If you are the invitee, insist on bringing something you can share.

We can view the Jewish community as a family of families. Wherever we find ourselves, we can branch out. If the ground is fertile, the new plantings will take root. Consider yourself your own outreach system, and no matter where you are on the observance spectrum, look to the left and to the right and see what you can share, what you have in common, who you can invite into your home, and who you can visit. Remember, you are not trying to change people, you are sharing yourselves, authentically.

Across the Jewish world, people are on the move. Generations may not share a worldview, they may be more or less religious, but people can reach out and get to know one another wherever they are. This is about people, not politics. Let your invitations come from your heart and allow that some people will be very accepting, and some will refuse. That's okay. Like a hummingbird finds the source of nectar in the garden, sprouts will find you. But be sure to plant those vines where they can be seen. Let your outside reflect who you are on the inside. Engage people warmly and openly everyday—don't wait till the night of the Seder!

Regardless of the health or age of a Green Bubbie, whatever she does have, she is able to share. You can be out on the tennis court, or at home in a wheelchair. Wherever you are, you can connect with others, see their value, and open the conversation. A Green Bubbie makes "the other" feel welcome.

A Green Bubbie knows how to listen, and how to begin the real conversations that connect us. These are the conversations that help us realize our potential as human beings, whatever worlds we are living in. She does not need to quote the *Times,* because her words are timeless. While I am personally somewhat of a news junkie, I have never seen the words *compassion, grace,* or *lovingkindness* in the morning paper. However, they do appear in daily Jewish prayer, repeatedly.

I believe there is an enormous amount of latent Bubbie power just waiting to be released. This timeless form of unconditional love may be just what our fragmented social landscape needs right now. Who wouldn't want to be greeted with a smile, to feel that someone is actually delighted to see us, someone we can turn to, someone who is not stressed out from work, someone who is, well, happy!

You have the power. Anoint yourself. Become a Green Bubbie; it is a gift only you can give to yourself, and it happens only by sharing yourself with others.

Three

Annuals to Evergreens

Rabbi Meir says, "Don't look at the jug, but rather at what is in it."
—Pirkei Avot (Ethics of the Fathers) 4:27

There is a discussion in *Pirkei Avot,* prior to Rabbi Meir's teaching, which is about what you can learn from an older teacher, versus a younger teacher. Rabbi Meir's teaching is preceded by Rabbi Yosi who says that learning from a young teacher can be compared to drinking wine from grapes that haven't even ripened and that learning from an older person is like drinking aged wine.

How can you tell who really has knowledge? Who has the teaching skills? Let's ask ourselves what Rabbi Meir is adding to this discussion in the teaching quoted at the beginning of this chapter. What is his warning for us? Don't look at the jug? What does that mean? It means don't be fooled by the externals, either of a jug, a wine barrel, or of people. And I would add plants as well. You can't tell what is within something without taking the time and effort to find out. Unlike the famous adage, "Don't judge a book by its cover," Rabbi Meir goes further. By telling us we must look inside, he is indicating that we have a moral imperative to look deeply, to investigate, to find out what is on the inside.

When you look at a garden in full bloom, you can't tell by looking what the provenance of a plant is. Was it planted from seeds? From heirloom seeds? Is it a hybrid? Perhaps it is a perennial that has been growing and increasing in size in this garden for years. How would you know if that beautiful red twig dogwood will be visible during the winter, or if it will wither to the ground? You can't tell just by looking at a garden how the plants got there or what they will need to thrive. You need to get to know each plant.

The same is true with people. Whether you walk into a half-empty synagogue, a bustling library, an overflowing gym, a painting class, or a playground, you can't assume anything about the people you meet. Don't assume everyone is in the same room for the same reason. When you see someone in your neighborhood, you can't tell how long she's lived there; you need to ask to find out.

Life in the garden is not linear. It is cyclical, with many different start times. Each plant grows at its own pace. To be a successful gardener, you need to know your plants, and you need to know yourself. The relationship between a garden and a gardener, like all relationships, changes over time.

We can learn from the garden how to ensure that there will be color and form all through the year, and in every season of our lives. The potential is there, we just have to plan for it. We also can learn that we have to work with nature to balance our own energies and strengths. In addition to planting food, we want to find spiritual sustenance in the garden. We can plant for fragrance, calm, and visual impact. I love to plant loofah sponges, yard-long beans, and birdhouse gourds that will attract children as well as butterflies, provoke conversation, and become the inspiration for my paintings. Think about what you want to attract.

One of the true joys of gardening is the planning, sometimes even more than the planting. And one of the best parts of winter is the arrival of the seed catalogs in January. If you have young children in your neighborhood, invite them over to "read" the seed catalogs with you. There is a world of potential stories to be written starring every variety of fruit, vegetable, and flower. You can make books, collages, and card games with the full-color pictures. If you know a young person who wants to garden, order a seed catalog to be delivered to their home. It is a free gift, and it can begin a priceless relationship.

First, let's consider annuals. These are the flowers that are planted each year. Although they are the brightest, longest-lasting blooms, they will die at the end of the season. A gardener who plants annuals has the unfailing belief that each year, no matter her level of strength, she will be able to plant new flowers in the garden.

From the annuals we can learn to relate to people as they are in each season. A Green Bubbie believes in the potential for growth, but she accepts people as they are now, in this season.

Accepting people and appreciating them for who they are *right now* is the key to healthy engagement. When I invite children to my garden, it is not because I think it will have an impact on their future. Their childhood is *now*. We are always growing, changing, aging, and so on. But in any given moment, we are who we are.

⌇

Perennials teach a different kind of faith. This is the faith that the plants will return in the next season. They disappear and lie dormant in the winter, with no sign of life, leaves, or stems. Sometimes I ask myself, "Where are those huge bushy plantings that were here last summer?" Sometimes I doubt myself. "Did I really plant them, or did I just think about planting them?" And then, in the spring, I see new signs of life, and by the summer I see so many of them even fuller and larger than ever. My memory still intact, my faith renewed.

You may not want to replant every year. Perhaps you are beginning to calculate the cost of annual flowers and decide you'd rather invest a bit more in perennials because they will come back every year. You may have the strength to plant, but you are beginning to appreciate the rewards of the garden doing its own work.

Perennials in the garden are somewhat akin to dividends from the stock market, only a bit more reliable. The real dividend of perennials is their constancy, reliability, and continuous growth. Perennial flowers reappear and you don't need to remember where you planted them. They will bloom, God willing, each year on their own—and what a great surprise and delight to see them! Ultimately, their real growth, like all growth, is out of our hands.

What can perennials teach us about people? They can teach us about the incremental process of growth and development. Real change does not happen overnight; it may take several "seasons." We can't force growth, and we can't change people.

⟜

Now let's talk about the evergreens. A garden in winter can be very bare. The evergreens keep their dark leaves, or pine needles, throughout the year. They provide strong structure, constancy of form, and function year-round.

The steadfastness and constancy of the evergreens reminds me of the Torah. In a world where everything changes, the truth of the Torah endures. No matter if the garden is in full bloom, with a magnificent array of colors, or if the dormancy of winter has left the garden gray, the evergreen stands firm. Sometimes it seems that it is where the contrasts are starkest—like the whitest snow of winter against the darkest green—that the presence of the evergreens is most visible.

The same Torah is learned by the very young and the very old. It isn't the Torah that changes. It is we who change. Our understanding of the words changes as we mature. The light shifts throughout the day; shadows are cast and images of trees appear to be rolling across the fallen snow, but the actual evergreen stands tall.

A Green Bubbie knows that Torah is eternal, and differing opinions, when offered "for the sake of Heaven," *LeShem Shamayim* (that is, for the purpose of deeper understanding rather than for argument's sake), are always welcome at her table.

With the help of her garden, a Green Bubbie understands deep in her "roots" that winter is not the end; it is the precursor of spring. The promise of new shoots and buds will be realized in the full bloom of summer. In fall, we gather the harvest and plan for the coming spring, and we preserve what we will need for winter.

There is a children's story by the writer and illustrator Leo Lionni, called *Frederik*. It is the story of a family of mice. One autumn all the mice go out to do their work preparing for the coming winter. Each mouse gathers nuts and seeds, and contributes to the building of a secure home for the coming winter. But Frederik seems to be doing no work—no gathering of nuts or seeds, no building. Frederik appears to be quietly gazing into the atmosphere. The other mice ask him what he is doing. Frederik replies that he is "gathering colors," which he will use to paint images in the coming dark, bleak months. He will use the colors to create the poems that will sustain the mice with vivid imagery throughout the cold, stark winter.

In my family, they call me Frederik. Frederik is, in fact, the Green Bubbie of the mouse world: collecting colors, gathering songs, humming melodies, teaching others to enjoy life in every season!

A Green Bubbie has absorbed the tradition she was born with or acquired along the way. It is a part of her and she has infused it into her home. Others bask in the light, color, and warmth when they visit. From the moment you enter her home, you know that it is more than a house. A house can be occupied and decorated; it can be sold or transferred. But a home is different. A home is transcendent, and what transpires there goes on for generations. A Green Bubbie creates just such an atmosphere. You can enter her home for an afternoon and leave with the keys to timeless tradition.

You can always welcome visitors to smell the flowers, eat the vegetables, listen to the birds, feel the breeze, or just join you for a cup of tea. You would be surprised at how many people are interested in a good conversation—even in the Quiet Car on the train!

A Green Bubbie nurtures with kindness and patience, and like companion plantings, she and her sprouts both grow, in their own ways, in their own seasons.

Four

Peas, Peas, P's

"My soul thirsts for the living God" Psalms 42:2

*B*ehold the humble pea. If you are thinking of frozen peas or canned peas, think again. In the garden there are many varieties of peas. However, there are two main categories that I would like to focus on, sweet peas and edible peas. Perennial sweet peas are beautiful, colorful flowers that, appear every year in the garden, covering everything with an intricate vine. They have a protrusion of beautiful delicate petals in pastel colors—pink, lavender, white. Annual sweet peas are not only beautiful but are intensely fragrant. While these two varieties provide endless pleasure for the senses, you cannot eat them. But, they serve a wonderful purpose of bringing beauty and joy to the garden.

The edible peas are another story. I plant them every year, and they are the first seeds to go into the garden. Actually, here in the Northeast where I live, St. Patrick's Day is the prime time for planting peas. There are bush peas, and climbing peas which need to be trellised. There are snow peas, snap peas, and pods of peas bursting with fullness. In our family, you are big enough to be a gardener as soon as you can stand on your own two feet without falling over the plants. By the time children are 15-to-18-months old, they can begin to toddle through the garden, and there is no better fine-motor activity for young children than to open a pea pod and pick out the peas. They are delicious, with a sweetness that you do not get from candy. I have found that one season of picking peas can establish a lifelong attachment to the garden!

The difference between the fragrant, beautifully colored sweet peas and the edible, delicious green ones provides an interesting opportunity to discuss another way our lives are divided, the physical and the spiritual. The physical world is the material world—the world of desire, of lust, of satisfying our urges, of focusing on the self. The physical is the body in which we live, and we have to eat or we will not live. The spiritual world is a world of feeling, of meta-cognition, of meaning-making, of looking beyond the self to the Creator. The spiritual world is where the soul connects to its maker, in a longing for closeness. We are beings who are both physical and spiritual; our task is to elevate the physical to the spiritual. Finding the balance in our lives between what we need to exist on a physical level and what we need to thrive on a spiritual level is our life's work.

So, there are edible plants, and there are plants that provide beauty for our senses and are meant to be appreciated but not eaten. It takes time to learn to live off the land, but you can learn easily with a knowledgeable guide. While this book is not a field guide to what we can eat in the garden, it is a field guide to what we can learn from the garden to satisfy our physical and spiritual needs.

During the Second World War, people planted "Victory Gardens." Victory Gardens fed the families of the soldiers. I would like to propose a Spiritual Victory Garden, to nourish sprouts, and feed the soul.

The Green Bubbie's Guide: How to Raise a Mensch.

I call it the 3 P's: People, Plants, Play. All are about relationships and responsibility. When you are needed you are not alone. People need involvement, caring, loving concern, and responsibility. We can teach the next generation that they are needed and important. Show them that we are happy to see them and that we all need each other. Plants depend on us to sustain their growth. Play is an essential part of living; it is the fuel to learning. As a Green Bubbie, if you can support the presence and growth of these 3 P's in your Spiritual Victory Garden, you will be doing your fair share to raise a generations of *menschen,* in your own front yard!

Creative, playful, and spiritual children become who they are by having creative, playful, and spiritual parents and grandparents. Start now! But remember: you cannot fake this. Enjoy the world, play in it; invite your sprouts to dig in with you.

Just as there is much planning that goes into planting seeds, raising someone to "mensch-hood" is no easy process. Before you even plant the first seeds in the ground, you have to prepare the soil. A famous rabbi was once asked, "At what age does a child's Jewish education begin? To which he answered, "Twenty years before he/she is born!" This is the spiritual DNA at work, as well as genetics and biology.

The public square has disappeared from many of our lives. Consider that you could be your own nonprofit for social change. Charge yourself with making the world a more friendly, welcoming place. Step out your front door, leave your comfort zone, and start smiling. As it says in Pirkei Avot 4:20, "Be the first to greet someone."

A Green Bubbie needs to be in the public domain. Get to know your neighborhood and neighbors. Start a conversation while in line at the grocery store, in synagogue, in your building's elevator, even on the train; greet people and get to know them. If you are a "sprout" of any age, say hello to a person who is older than you; get to know each other!

I am an artist. Frequently parents of young children will ask if their children can have art lessons. I would rather spend the time on creating art than teaching it. But I do like children, and I don't mind at all if a few of them want to come over and paint with me. They can bring their own supplies, and spend time quietly painting if they want to be with a real artist. I like sharing that part of myself. Sometimes, children want to come and work or play in my garden. I love that, too. I can teach them to weed, rake, or dig. I can share the berries, and they can take home any carrots, kale, or tomatoes that they pull or pick. But there is never any financial transaction.

Painting and gardening are my passions. I enjoy sharing them and am enriched by the presence of young children (and their parents) appreciating the skills I am cultivating. I am also showing the children that there are relationships and transactions that have nothing to do with money.

Sometimes I get calls from parents of older children inquiring about art lessons, and I know they really mean, "Help, this kid is driving me crazy!" In the rearing of children, context is everything. Sometimes by changing the context, we see a very different child. When I can, I like to suggest that the child come over to help in the garden, or work with me in the studio. I do not do this as a tutor or therapist. If I can spend an hour or even an afternoon with a young person, to provide another relationship, I like to do so; it is a *chesed*, an act of kindness. I insist on no payment.

I think we need to give children an honest message. Children can tell when their parents are paying for someone to spend time with them. If you want a child to feel valued for himself, he needs to know you are not being paid to spend time with him. All of us know when someone is sharing him- or herself with us. The same child who is driving her mother nuts may be the model of concentration and good manners in my studio.

Over the past decade or two, giving advice has become an industry, and asking for help a pathology. Sometimes people just want to talk—not by appointment, and not for a 50-minute hour. People want to get to know one another, to learn the lessons others have learned in their lives.

A Green Bubbie can sew together a patchwork of individuals and families into a tapestry far more complex and strong. When a Green Bubbie greets a young child or nourishes a local sprout, she is not adopting anyone into her own family. This is not about building a personal legacy. On the contrary, when a Green Bubbie reaches out or down to hold the hand of a very young child, she is doing so as a representative of the community. Essentially, she is the Jewish community's Bubbie-at-Large.

"Fiddler on the Roof" perpetuated the narrative that tradition was something that we needed to break away from, as opposed to seeing it as the very thing that supports us. There has been a confusion concerning the ever-changing cultural contexts in which we find ourselves and the truths of Torah, which are timeless. One of the strengths of Judaism is that it is transmitted from one generation to the next, often at the dining-room table. But what if the food served at a table is meant only for the body? What happens to those who live with full stomachs but empty hearts and thirsty souls?

There is an emotional ecology at work here. People gravitate to one another. Where there is a healthy mutual admiration, a scaffolding supportive network can grow. From. companion planting, we have learned which plants grow well together, we see that roses grow well with garlic. In the garden, combining a variety of particular plants creates a synergistic power, which results in a healthier, pest-free climate.

When everyone is the same age, as when there is only one kind of plant in the garden, there is a potential risk from unknown factors. In a monoculture, where there is no diversity, a single fungus can wipe out the whole crop at once, like the potato famine in Ireland. When there is a homogeneity of any one factor, there is risk from insularity.

A Green Bubbie can insert herself into a monoculture to diversify it just by being herself. For instance, when a sprout is busy at work and everyone around her has the same stresses, she can forget the importance of looking up from her computer and taking a break in the middle of the day. Sometimes what's needed is a text message from a Green Bubbie saying, "Hey, do you want to meet at the art museum to have lunch with Kandinsky and me?"

The Green Bubbie and her sprouts are generationally complimentary! Grown in different eras, they gravitate to a "cultural point" somewhere on life's spiritual journey. We don't grow in isolation. We thrive in organic diversity. We are interconnected with Torah, the natural world, and with one another.

For seeds to take root and sprout, one of the best soils is a loose mixture of composted materials, vermiculite, and peat moss. I use the "recipe" outlined by Mel Bartholomew in his books on Square Foot Gardening. Why should the soil be loose? Well, imagine you are a carrot and your job is to grow under ground. If the soil is hard and unwelcoming, there is no room to spread out your roots. If you are a carrot, you *are* your root! There is no room for a growing carrot (or parsnip, onion, beet—you know *root* vegetables!) to spread out and grow fully. A root vegetable can't reach its potential in a hard, unforgiving environment.

What do children need to grow? I believe that children need emotional warmth, recognition of their individuality, healthy friendships, and spiritual direction. The Native Americans learned that corn, beans, and squash grow best when planted together, and they gave a name to this trio: they called them "The Three Sisters." Jews do not grow in isolation; to reach one's potential, children and adults alike need a supportive social context.

I believe that a community can be a rich mix of nutrients in which children can be supported and able to stretch out their roots to reach their full potential. Like a loose mix of soil in a garden, there is room for everyone to grow according to his particular needs. As it says, "Teach a young child according to his ways and he will not depart from it [Torah] when he is older." Proverbs 22:6

So, how does a Green Bubbie support the early growth process? She becomes an ingredient in the fertile soil into which children develop. This well-balanced mix includes the language, stories, foods, cultural narrative, and classical texts (the Torah) of Judaism. And it includes people in the community who reach out to you. This becomes the fertile soil from which the young grow and learn.

Teaching Torah values to very young children gives them "innoculents"—just like that stuff we mix with peas and beans to ensure their strong early growth. Just as plants need to be scaffolded on a strong support, a child's spiritual life, if begun early, becomes the skeletal structure onto which the rest of life's experiences can grow and be nourished. A strong spiritual backbone becomes the focal point of the moral compass a person needs in life. Children need to be taught Jewish values not only from books, but from people who are living by the Book!

All the learning in the world is only words until you experience the values being lived. The tradition of rising in the presence of a great rabbi is not to afford honor to the person, but rather, to honor all the Torah the person has learned. We stand in the presence of one who has made the Torah a part of their whole being. A child will grow in a place of Torah if there are people surrounding that child who she can look up to and recognize as the embodiment of all that learning. This is not esoteric knowledge; it is action. It is the life of a community of kindness, a holiness that demonstrates self-respect, and respect for others.

So open your Green Bubbie home, your heart, and your garden. Share your life. Feed the soul.

Five

Moonlight in the Garden

It is good to sing praises to the Lord,
to recount Your goodness in the morning
and Your faithfulness at night. —Psalm 92

Much of gardening happens in the early morning. Before the heat of the day, gardeners are outside working the land. But appreciating the garden happens even when the sun goes down. The shade—the absence of sun—is also necessary.

Evening in the garden is serene, with fragrant breezes from the phlox, the roses, and the peonies. If you want your garden to sparkle in the dark, plant flowers with bright white petals. Just as there are morning glories of intense color, which open up early in the day, there are moon flowers that unfurl *their* blossoms, lighting up the night.

The same garden is different at different times of the day. The artist Claude Monet painted to capture the effects of light on his garden in Giverny. To appreciate the fullness of life, we need to see it in all kinds of light.

Gardening pulls our attention to the ground itself. The Holy One designated humankind as the stewards of the earth, but the first mitzvah that He gave to the Jewish people was to bless the new moon. In other words, "Look up!"

God commanded us to bless the moon, putting into our hands the power to sanctify time, to set the times for the holidays and the months in their cycles. This is an opportunity to join in a sacred partnership—a covenant—that says we take on the responsibility for making life holy. In Jewish thinking, time *is* life; it is precious. Use it well.

The Talmud teaches, "Whoever blesses the new moon in its time invites the *Shechina*, God's presence, to dwell within." That power is yours. Get to know the moon in its cycles. In the Sabbath preceding the beginning of each new Hebrew month, we pray that God will bless us with "long life, a life of peace, a life of goodness, a life of sustenance... a life in which all of our innermost questions will be answered for the good." By reciting this timeless prayer, you become focused on what is important, and worth praying for. You can add your own prayers as well.

Blessing the new moon is something a Green Bubbie can do in her own, unique way. Imagine having a list of people of varying ages who you intentionally call once a month—on Rosh Chodesh—just to wish them a *gitten chodesh; a chodesh tov;* or, in English, a good month! What could happen? First of all, your days would be counted differently, as you'd begin to focus on the Hebrew calendar. You would have something special to look forward to on a regular basis. You wouldn't feel alone and neither would your sprouts—everyone involved would feel extra love on that day. Perhaps you would like to bake moon cookies and share them. Maybe on Rosh Chodesh you could invite a few other Green Bubbies over to chat, to learn, to do a little gardening.

As we witness the continual "disappearance" and return of the moon, our faith is strengthened with each cycle. We sense that God's goodness in the world is there, even when things look dark. We know what is real. God's presence, like the moon, is sometimes hidden, sometimes revealed, but always there.

Like the moon, a Green Bubbie isn't always physically present, but she is there if needed, and her sprouts know it. This can create an enormous sense of confidence and peace of mind. I tell a few of my sprouts that I am here in case of emergency—never on a regular basis, but as a backup, for that day when they need help. I have let parents of young children know that I am here if they need me in the middle of the night, or if an emergency takes them out of town. So far there have been a few close calls, but I have had only one little boy as a "guest." I like to think the parents are holding their "Get Out of Jail Free" card, just in case.

⌣‒

We can all use someone a few years ahead of us to help think things through. The comfort and power of knowing that someone is listening to you, caring about you—especially someone who might have experienced or have knowledge about something you're going through—reminds us that we are not alone. Rooted conversations between generations have been a treasured link between grandparents and their grandchildren for time immemorial.

The Green Bubbie is a hyperlink in these conversations. When you begin to tell her something, in the blink of an eye you can tell if you've touched a chord. By encouraging you to dig deeper, she can help you uncover your own motivations, your own desires beneath the good news you had intended to share. We are really good at storytelling, giving tantalizing bits of news, but what about the hidden meanings? You can fool yourself into thinking that if you are really busy, your life is full. A Green Bubbie can help you differentiate between a life that is full and a life of fulfillment.

A Green Bubbie is not in a hurry. She can perceive nuanced transitions in nature. Just as she sees the first appearance of the tiny sliver of a new moon, she appreciates the tiniest sparks of originality and individuality in people. We can all learn to recognize the spark of potential in others. A Green Bubbie can zoom in on the essence of a person and on the essential qualities of nature. She sees the world through what I call the "Magical Green Bubbie Viewfinder"—the power of infinite observation, permanently set on "auto nonjudgmental."

Perhaps you remember fireflies from your childhood (maybe you called them lightning bugs), which you caught and put in a jar with holes poked into the top to give them air. If you go outside on a warm summer night those fireflies are still lighting up. But not everything is the same as it used to be. Robert Louv, in his insightful book *The Last Child in the Woods*, documents the disappearance of the actual woods and wildlife, and the resultant negative effects on children. If you have been thinking that you don't see as much greenery as you did in your childhood, you're right! Suburban sprawl, development, and city ordinances have all resulted in less wilderness and wildlife accessible from residential areas. What's more, children are more "plugged in," preferring the indoors and digital frontiers to the outdoors and the woods. But experiential learning requires the child to actually have experiences. You can Google the sound of a gurgling stream, but you can't feel the water or the rush of the current.

A Green Bubbie can open the door back into the wilderness. Follow me outside: start with the porch, the deck, the window, and reorient yourself and those around you. If you want to preserve the environment, first you have to get to know it, fall in love with it, and then you will become passionate about saving it.

You can hone your skills as a spiritual tour guide just by asking the right questions. For instance, going on vacation? Are you thinking Orlando or Utah? Would you like to give your children the opportunity to shake hands with a "real" animated character, to see a "real" version of their fantasy world? Or, would you like to give them a fantastic vision of the "real world" beyond what they could ever imagine—the mountains, the craters, the canyons, the oceans?

You don't need to sleep in a tent to see our wondrous national parks and seashores (I'm talking to you, camping-averse Green Bubbie!)—you can stay in your car and take the scenic drive and stay in a motel! No matter where you live or travel, be the one who points out the window. Whether you go to the Catskills, the Poconos, or the Rockies, take your eyes off the iPad and lift them up to the mountains! The green of the Northeast is nothing like the red rocks of the West, and the Grand Canyon is called that for a very good reason. Explore, enjoy, and be totally awed by the wonder of it all.

Life goes quickly. One moment you look at a baby and decide she is too young for the beach. Then you blink and you can't believe she's ten and she's never seen an ocean! The most energy-efficient lesson you can give about spirituality and the environment is that it is never far from where you are. Go outside and get to know the world, now!

⌒

Turn your emotional energy into spiritual power!

The special secret of a Green Bubbie is that she knows how to turn emotional energy into spiritual power, and how to turn that spiritual power into emotional energy when needed! That spiritual power is Judaism's teaching that we have control over our time, our emotions, and our desires. We have free choice, and that includes choosing to make our emotions subservient to our will.

The secret is to take all that emotional energy that could go into worrying about everything and trying to exert control, and instead, let go. Just...let... go. Release your own love into the universe and have faith that it is God who is in control. Try recalling all those things you've ever worried about: Did your worrying do anything? Change anything? How much energy have you expended holding your breath waiting for a phone call, for the arrival of loved ones, for a letter of acceptance or rejection? It turns out that worry is not the essential feature of being a Jewish mother. The essential feature is faith.

The key for turning emotional energy into spiritual power is expressed in the mitzvah, *to be happy.* Mitzva Gedolia Lihiot B'Simcha "It is a great Mitzvah to be in a state of happiness." Sounds simple, right? But a **great** mitzvah, may at the same time, be a **hard** mitzvah. It is not always easy to be *"b'Simcha"* but I have found that by training myself to recognize the good, to find what to be grateful for, to search and see the kindness of The Holy One, even in the midst of tragedy, hardship, illness and the death of loved ones, has enabled me to develop into a person of enduring faith and belief beyond the parameters of my own finite life.

We can never really know what God has in mind, but if we can live with the belief that there is ultimately good, it becomes our task to find it, and to hold that as our ultimate reality. We may have to look long and hard, but faith is knowing that good is there. This is not an easy idea, or an obvious truth, but I have found it to be true in my life.

Like the moon's light, we are continually in a process of renewal. Renewal is different than searching for the fountain of youth. A Green Bubbie doesn't strive to be young or young again. She blossoms in that light of renewal, from the inside out!

Six

Compost Yourself

"With compassion, the Holy One, Illuminates the Earth and All who Dwell within, And in His goodness, continuously renews the work of creation, each and every Day." —Jewish daily morning prayer

*I*n the material world, growth is a continuum, a process leading to eventual decay. In the spiritual world, the opposite is true; a person is always capable of continuous growth, learning, and refinement of character. Just as the Holy One, in His goodness, each day continually renews the work of Creation, we too have the opportunity to renew ourselves- each and every day!

Composting is about life, not death, so relax when I suggest that you "compost yourself." Composting for the Green Bubbie is not the same as decomposing. If you are actively composting yourself, you are very much alive. In fact, we will see how life gives life through composting.

Composting in the garden is the process of recycling organic material into fertile soil. It involves using scraps from raw foods and combining them with organic matter from the garden. With the infusion of plenty of water, and turning the layers of food and garden scraps, they combine into a new incredibly nutrient rich compound. It is the ultimate recycling process.

In the Talmud, the section of the Mishna, called Zeraim (seeds) focuses on Jewish agricultural laws. Essentially there are three categories of Torah law mandating us to remember the poor when farming the land- Leket, Shich'cha, and Peah. All have to do with separating what is kept by the owner and what is left over, given away. Leket is the amount of the harvest which is inadvertently dropped while harvesting. Shich'cha is the sheaves that have been forgotten during the harvesting, which is then forbidden to be re-claimed. 'Peah' refers to a corner- a section of a field which is left unharvested, intentionally set aside for the poor. The issue is separating what we keep from what is left for others. The essential teaching is that nothing is really ours alone.

As a metaphor, what can we learn from these Jewish agricultural laws that could apply to the idea of composting ourselves? In all areas of life, even as it pertains to the land, the Torah teaches that we have obligations to others. Even the wheat in our fields, doesn't belong to us- we are obligated to give a portion away to those less fortunate. In our own lives, what really belongs to us- and what can we give away?

What do we accumulate in the course of a life time that can be used, transferred or re-purposed? When we look at ourselves, are we defined by what we have, or by what we are? Are we known by what we own, or by what we do with what we have?

Don't start saving your coffee grounds; remember, for our purposes, composting is a metaphor. The message is that as you revisit the experiences you've had in your life, you can appreciate which have been formative, instructive, essential, or meaningful. This is not a memory of things past, it is the realization of who you have become. You are the vessel of your learning. When a sprout meets you, she sees your life through her eyes. It is your life that becomes the fertile ground to support her future.

⟳

What transforms us and how do we keep growing? In the spiritual realm, growth and change are positive. In the physical world there is fear and resistance to age. It would be good if we could trust the world we live it. However, we are all too familiar with the lure of the world of illusion, hypocrisy, and falsehood. There is a multi-billion dollar business for 'anti-aging' products. Am I the only one that finds this puzzling? Is everybody else walking down the up staircase?

Green Bubbie is not anti-aging. Green Bubbie is about positive aging. Generative aging! Truth in advertising! Let's unite- get on the truth train, full speed ahead. Our job isn't to show that we can *reverse* the signs of aging, our job is to program our GPS to take the scenic route.

When my father A"H turned 90, it was a difficult year. For the first time in his life I think he was depressed. He was living with us and my then twelve year old son suggested, lovingly, that he might be having an 'old age crisis.' At the time an unusual number of red sports cars had begun to populate our neighborhood so the idea of age related crises was a familiar theme. Nothing seemed to help until my older son sat down with his beloved grandfather and said, "Zayda, all your life you were a teacher, now you have to teach us how to be 90." Well, that was the turning point, and the beginning of one of best and most positive years of his life. In fact, on his death bed, a nurse whispered softly to ask if he knew his blood type- to which my father thrust his fist in the air and with a tremendous smile proclaimed, "B Positive."

The entertainment industry has tried to convince us that no one wants to look at older people- women in particular. But it isn't the case that no one is looking—the truth is *everyone* is looking! We have a responsibility to look as good as we can, and to be as good as we can. We need to set a great example, because EVERYBODY is looking, and they are all aging — getting older is a privilege.

I don't think I have ever received a greater compliment than when I hear my Sprouts say that they would like to be like me when they get older. WHAT? I always need a moment to compose myself. It is easy to forget that these sprouts that I like so much really are young enough to be my children. I wonder for a moment what it is that they see in me. Most of them have more money in their young lives than I will ever accumulate in mine. Many of them have advanced degrees and fabulous professions, families, freedoms, and great talents.

What do they see in me? I think they see someone who is interested in them. I am someone with a life of my own, with creative passions and yet time for other people. I think they see in me someone who cares about what's going on in *their* lives—even though we aren't related. I invite them for meals or coffee, just them, or with their families. Mostly, I think they like conversations and honest sharing of experiences- stories of religious journeys, child rearing strategies, educational choices, how to get along with in-laws or bosses, and the pros and cons of second careers, life as an artist, a great book suggestion and of course the best time to plant seeds. I send text greetings before holidays or random check ins. Just a "Hi, I am thinking of you."

I think my life as an artist and gardener is a testament that there is creativity and great joy after the kids get older, after the great job, and well before the sun sets. Sprouts want to know that there is life after their kids leave preschool even before they can even imagine that future.

Turn yourself inside out. Check that your actions and your values are one and the same. If you are living the life you believe in, when people meet you, they recognize your authenticity. When someone says "I want to be like you." you'll know what they mean. Sift through your life and make sure that what people see is what you are. Being a Green Bubbie is organic, not only is it natural–there are no hidden layers or ulterior motives.

I think people also like advice- especially if it is about how to become a Green Bubbie in the future. (Be a BIT:Bubbie in Training!) Advice for sprouts: Don't throw out all of your kid's toys, save those Beany Babies. Teach your children that other children matter too, and that if you save their toys, younger children who visit will play with them. Warning: when your child complains they don't want to go somewhere because there won't be anyone their age, help them to appreciate what they can learn and give to people who are younger or older. We live in a very age-segregated society, take every opportunity you can to break out of that narrow view of life. Even young children can learn nurturing behaviors, and kindness; a first step on the road to compassionate, inter-generational living.

One of the current trends in sustainable agriculture is permaculture. One of the essential features of permaculture is observation. Observe the environment and learn from it. Get to know your garden over time to see the effects of sunlight and shade. Get to know how the seasons will affect your garden. Pay attention.

So too with people, community, and cultures. Pay attention. First get to know yourself. What do you value? What are your interests, strengths, passions? What about you do you want to share with others? Observe "the other." Get to know her.

There is a common gardening adage that goes something like this: One man's weeds is another man's lunch! Don't assume that everything, or even anything you have, will be valued by someone else. Who are the people who you feel most comfortable with? Who can you learn from? With whom are you most likely to share the best of you?

Sometimes in the garden the soil is lacking in an essential nutrient. Adding the rich compost can balance out the soil to nourish new plants. So too in community. A composted Bubbie can add a different dimension or perspective to enrich the sprout or community with a special, essential ingredient.

In the material world, if we are missing something, we can search for it. In the spiritual world, we don't necessarily know what we are looking for. We may feel a void, but until we see something in another person, you can't necessarily name what you are seeking. When I see someone who is calm and peaceful, I am in awe. I am always drawn to people who put family first, and exhibit an inner peace that seems to set them apart from the material trappings of society.

A Green Bubbie and her sprouts are generationally complimentary. Grown in different eras, they gravitate to each other. You recognize each other as fellow travelers.

When you "compost yourself" you move beyond the labels and choices that society has foisted upon women. The choices of work/family balance are seen for what they really are: simplistic, confining categories of women's lives.

These are popular but limiting images of how we can define ourselves. Our lives have so much more meaning and potential. Relationships provide depth and definition and build communities that maximize our human potential. We are more than "bread winners" when we work, and more than "child-care providers" to our children. Life takes time.

You *can* have it all, it just takes a life time. Don't be tempted to force every experience into one time frame.

⟨⟩

Regardless of where we are on the economic scale we can share ourselves with another human being, grow in compassion, and gain in wisdom. When a compost pile, filled with plant and organic materials recombines, a tremendous amount of heat is produced to energize the conversion process.

A key ingredient to powering your future is sustained purpose. Stay focused on what you care deeply about, and that sustained purpose will energize your transformation, it will power your growth.

I believe that there is an emotional drought in our world brought about by hyper focusing on our own needs and self interests. Life is with people, There is an isolation that has resulted from decades of not talking to strangers. As adults, if you don't talk to strangers, how will you make new friends?

Parents don't have to battle each other as the only two people who can care for and about their kids. I know that when there is shared purpose whether it is a common religious community, an artistic, agricultural, or neighborhood district, when people care about each other, family and work become just two among many variables that create a balanced life. Rather than a see-saw, a one point fulcrum where one or the other is winning, we can re-imagine the equation and expand the limiting 50/50 work/family calculation.

What if we imagine a Calder mobile art sculpture, where "work" and "family" are only two of multiple components of our attention and identity. In this new image, work and family are not in conflict with each other, vying for supremacy. What if we include the arts, the outdoors, leisure, gardening, religion, or music as all essential variables. Imagine working and raising a family for a greater purpose, being part of a larger community of shared values and interests.

It is easy to think of an older person as representing the past—but no! A Green Bubbie is fascinating because she represents a version of the future! The more positive role models you have ahead of you, the brighter the future appears. When you are that role model, your life, gives life.

We have an opportunity to give birth to our own children. We also have an opportunity to make of our own lives models that can give birth to new imaginative possibilities for other people's lives. When someone says they want to be like you, chances are that they see that you are still growing, and that is the most life affirming vision of the future you can provide.

A Green Bubbie lives the potential of the Future!

Pray for Rain

Rabbi Akiva says: *"Everything is foreseen,*
Yet, freedom of choice is granted;
The world is judged with goodness,
And everything is according to the preponderance of action."

—*Pirkei Avot, Chapter 5*

*e*ven if you've never planted a garden, you can still appreciate that rain is a blessing, and *that* is a blessing in itself.

If there were a severe drought, it might be easy to pray for rain. But on a beautiful, clear day, when the garden is lush, what is there to pray for? When the tomatoes on the vine turn red as they ripen, it is easy to take credit for having planted them in just the right sunlight. But the more experienced the gardener, the more she knows how much is beyond her own skill-set. All you can do is keep the soil healthy, weed, mulch, and plant. Sun, shade, and rain are the essentials. To garden is to continually learn that life is ultimately out of our control.

There is nothing like the life of a gardener to keep one grounded. Yet, there is nothing more spiritual, either. Where did God first "plant" us? In a garden, the Garden of Eden. That act set the course for the relationship between God and humankind. God shows His faith in us by making us the stewards of His garden, and we show our faith in God by planting and praying for the rain that is God's blessing.

There is a spiritual interrelationship between God, the universe, and us: we are in this together! God asks us to activate the growth of the physical universe by praying for rain. What do we need to do to activate our spiritual growth? Our Tradition gives us an encouraging hint, "Open for Me a hole the size of an eye of a needle, and I will open for you an opening the size of a grand hall." *Midrash Shir HaShirim* If we take a small first step, God will respond beyond measure.

My father, A"H, used to say that he loved to walk in the rain because he thought of the rain drops as kisses from God. There is an expression, *Geshmei Bracha*, the rains of blessing. A gardener knows that we can do everything possible to make a garden grow, but only God can make it rain. Feeling the rain, feeling God's blessings touching us, is the beginning of acknowledging a very personal relationship with our Creator.

Women have always had a unique way of praying. The Torah has numerous examples of women's personal prayers. In song and in eloquent prose, with tears and with silence, the prayers from the hearts of women have filled the narrative of our Jewish history.

It would be easy to simply mirror the world of men's prayer with its quorum of ten men. I would like to suggest an alternative. Perhaps the Green Bubbie could offer a uniquely Jewish mode of woman's prayer—I call it "parallel pray."

There is a concept in child development known as "parallel play." A child encounters another child in the sandbox and they begin to play alongside each other, with no expectation of interaction or engagement. As they become aware of each other's actions, through observation, imitation, and small gestures, they continue to play in the sand, not necessarily together, but in sync, with a developing awareness of each other.

In parallel pray, I envision women occasionally sharing moments of reverence, observing the style, manner, sounds, and choreography of another woman's prayer life. I learned to read Hebrew in a Hebrew school; I learned to pray by being around other women who actually prayed! And I only learned that you could pray on your own from observing my women friends who prayed at various times of the day in their own homes—and sometimes in hospital rooms.

Every morning I go outside, prayerbook in one hand, coffee in the other. I have a swing on my porch surrounded by my gardens. Sometimes I invite a friend over to *daven* (pray) with me. We learn from each other. Sometimes we sit on the porch observing the time frame and cadences of each other's *davening*. One friend remarked that it had never occurred to her to take her time and to take breaks, so to speak. We shared another pattern: first *daven brachos* (the early morning blessings), then eat breakfast, and then continue the rest of the morning prayers. I mentioned that I learned that from observing my daughter and daughters-in-law, in their homes!

If so much of a woman's personal prayers happen in the privacy of her home, how can we learn from one another? From my own mother, A"H, I learned that I could have an ongoing dialogue with God. She had a direct line to the *Ribonno Shel Olam*, the Creator of the Universe. Throughout the day and night, she used her own personal prayers as needed. But I did not grow up in a home where saying *Tehillim* (Psalms) was a daily practice, and I had no experience of watching my mother sitting and praying with a prayer book. I now am a person who prays at home, and I have grandchildren who can learn from me, but that is only because I have met many women who believe in the power of prayer and of the healing process in the saying of psalms.

When I was diagnosed with cancer many years ago, someone gave me a book by Rabbi Matisyahu Solomon, called *With Hearts Full of Faith*. In it he taught that prayer doesn't change God's mind, it changes the one who prays.

Since reading those words, I pray differently. I pray to become the kind of person who can handle life as it happens. I have morphed into a person of faith, from a person who used to worry. And I have learned that I can pray fervently for the health and welfare of my family and friends, and I pray for them by name. I don't know if any of the lives of my friends or family were prolonged as a result of my prayers. I can tell you it deepened our relationships, and it stretched me. I never knew I could care so deeply and commit to doing all that I could on their behalf.

I can you tell how grateful I remain for all those who prayed for me when I was ill, some of whom still mention my name in their prayers. I can tell you that as I prayed with all my heart for the lives of others, they remain in my consciousness, they are a part of me, of the person I became as I prayed for them.

Sometimes, I like to leave the comfort of my front porch and go into the gardens in the back of the house for prayer, meditation, and a closer look at the trees. I have a friend whose children are Bratslaver Chassidim; she joins me in the garden and we spend time praying, *davening* in and out of the formulated prayers. Together we wonder about our children's lives, our own lives, the meaning of the words, as we follow the light in the trees. We listen and take note of the breeze.

A Green Bubbie is blessed with various means of communication and expression. Her message is personal and her medium can range from music and art to prayer and contemplation, with coffee, wine, or chocolate as the situation demands.

Imagine that "The Green Bubbie" is a yoga position. Stretch out your arms as far as you can. *Now hold that pose!* Imagine all the people you could touch, care about, invite to your garden or to your Shabbat table. Now, exhale and... invite them! Can you feel your power?

If you think the magic wand in the hands of Cinderella's fairy godmother was powerful, consider this: a Green Bubbie has the power to make time holy! You could shop 'til you drop, or you could stop and say, "Wait! It's Friday and the sun is setting. The Sabbath Queen is about to enter. I can transform my home into a palace in time; I can set a table with silver and fine china for a sumptuous feast by candlelight." Move over Downton Abbey! The Green Bubbie like every Jewish woman, has the power to elevate her home for one whole day every week; elevate her life, her family, and her friends by connecting them with the ultimate Source of royalty.

The fascination we all have with the "haves and the have-nots" is the monetary expression of opposites, like the division between the sacred and the profane. Regardless of your economic status, Shabbos is what enables everyone on every level to make a distinction between the mundane week and the beautiful holiness of the Sabbath Day. Save the best food, the sweets, the best wine, the best clothes for this one special day. It doesn't matter how much you have, it matters that whatever you have, you save the best of it for Shabbos.

Start early each week looking forward to that one day that is not about us; it is about something more important than any of us. When the Sabbath Queen enters your home, transport yourself to the palace and allow yourself a "taste of the World to Come." Give yourself the gift of a spiritual pleasure cruise, connect with *your* Creator. Experience complete rest, become renewed, start a clean slate with a new week, refreshed, spiritually recharged.

Shabbos is a time to focus on the spiritual light—to turn off the electricity, decrease our carbon footprint, stay local, and rest; to appreciate family and friends; to recharge our spiritual batteries. A Green Bubbie knows that in blessing the Sabbath candles she brings holiness into her home. Every Jewish woman who lights the Sabbath candles has learned it from another Jewish woman—this is the ultimate Green Bubbie experience, to learn and to teach. The learning is 24/7, but the times and places are sacred.

The Green Bubbie's wisdom is *hakarat hatov,* recognizing the good, expressing gratitude for God's goodness. She has come to value every minute of life, not because it is fleeting, but because she is open to its enormity. A Green Bubbie cherishes all of God's creations, taking on her responsibility to perfect the world and refine her life.

The greater our understanding of the magnitude of God's blessings, the greater our appreciation of God's Kindness (*Chasdei Hashem*) and the more we want to share that kindness. When a Green Bubbie shares her wisdom with you it is the opposite of a copyright; if there is a new idea, she wants you to take it and run with it! When the baton is passed, the whole relay team wins.

We Green Bubbies know that the gift we have, of being *able* to love, is what we emulate of God's love for us. It is the source of our continuing strength. We recognize our place in the link of tradition. We know what we have received, and we want to share it. We are aware from our own level of learning how much more there is to learn. We accept doubt, yet we are well on our way to belief.

Each of us has a spiritual faith tradition. Mine is the Jewish tradition, and learning Torah is empowering me, energizing me to grow more fully, to seek the peace that is completion and wholeness. The more I understand the idea that God created the world to show His love for us, the more I am compelled to find more ways to show my love for others.

We have come to know that rain is a physical manifestation of God's blessings. We can feel it, and we can't live without it. We can choose to feel the spiritual rains of God's blessings.

Just as a Green Bubbie cares for other people's sprouts as well as her own, so, too, when she prays for rain, it's not just for her garden.

May we all be showered with God's blessings as we humbly tend the Garden. Together.

Epilogue

A few weeks after my mother died, I received a call from her very good friend Florence. My mother had so many close friends, and, as her daughter, I treasured the uniqueness of our own relationship. I knew even then that there are some things you can share only with your friends, and other things that are for just your immediate family.

When Florence called, I was eager to hear what she had to say, especially when she prefaced it with, "You know what a sense of humor your mother had?" I wasn't sure if she was asking or confirming information about this very funny woman. My mother had made a final request, and as her best friend, Florence was about to carry it out.

You can imagine my reaction when Florence said, "Your mother made me promise that I would call you occasionally to remind you to take the lint out of the dryer."

"TAKE THE LINT OUT OF THE DRYER!" This is a legacy?

As it turned out, every time Florence called me, I did need to take the lint out of the dryer. Months after my mother's death, I called Florence to tell her I was just thinking of her, and that she need not worry about me setting the house on fire. My mother had probably told her of my limited housekeeping skills. As a result, Florence continued to call about the lint.

Over the next few years, I got to know Florence. I used to take my children to visit "MomMom's friend Florence," and during those visits she would recount all of the funny things my mother would say over the course of their long friendship; all sorts of great memories were shared, and Florence was continually interested in our lives. Florence became part of my family, and we developed an intergenerational friendship. Florence gave voice to the memory of my mother, and provided a welcome presence in that incredible void left within me.

After many years, I realized that my mother's final request to her dear friend—"Please call Ruth every once and a while to remind her to take the lint out of the dryer"—had nothing to do with the laundry. She had bequeathed to me a relationship—with a Green Bubbie! She had found a way to ensure that there would be a caring force in my life, even after hers.

Share your self, and your presence and your love will continue, not only for your life, but into the lives of those you love.

In a world where we are all engaged in important efforts to secure our finances and ensure our health care, we sign documents to assign legal guardianship and designate our power of attorney.

Now, consider your life and what you really value. Remember the tradition you have received and that you are empowered to transmit. And then, no matter where you are in your life, consider becoming, or finding, a Green Bubbie.

Exercise your *power of eternity*!

Acknowledgements

When I think of all the people who have contributed to the writing of *The Green Bubbie,* the list would be longer than the book itself! But I would be remiss in not singling out a few individuals whose enthusiasm and support of the idea behind the book gave me the courage to go forward with it.

When *The Green Bubbie* was in its formative stage, I shared the idea with illustrator Chris Muller and his wife, costume designer Constance Hoffman. Over lunch, Constance shared that her professional life had been influenced by her Italian aunt and grandmother, both seamstresses who allowed her to play as a child with spools of thread and beautiful fabrics. In retrospect, they were, of course, Green Bubbies! Before we finished lunch, *The Green Bubbie's* wardrobe was being designed by Constance, and images were already taking shape in Chris's imagination. I thank him now for the incredible Cover Design of this book.

Throughout my life, I have been blessed with many women who have been role models, friends, and teachers. My mother died when I was in my thirties. At my mother's funeral, Dr. Marciene Mattleman, a friend and mentor, came up to me and assured me that she would "be there for me." And Marciene *has* been there for me, and has celebrated the birthdays of my children and stood with me at all of my family's life-cycle events. She is an educator and professor of education, and has been a caring and important role model for me. After retiring from her university job, she went on to form five successful nonprofit organizations to benefit the children of Philadelphia. Marciene is a Green Bubbie in our civic society, and has always planted seeds for children's potential growth. She has a wonderful family of her own, yet she has found the time and energy to care for so many others. She has shared her true self, her heart, with so many others, not least of all with me.

When I first began to talk about the idea of the Green Bubbie, it was not clear to me whether it should be an organization or a commodity. I am profoundly grateful to my friends in the foundation world who nurtured and approved of my ideas—from the very first when Terry Rubinstein said of the Green

Bubbie, "This has legs...go with it." Judith Ginsburg confirmed with enthusiasm how many people could really consider themselves Green Bubbies and what a reach the idea could have. Rachel Levin encouraged me to pursue my real strengths, which she reminded me were my faith and my understanding of the the importance of relationships. Lisa Brill's commitment to family and friends is a testament to how to live lovingly in this world. These women set the stage for *The Green Bubbie* by continually sharing themselves as well as their wisdom. Their faith in what I could accomplish has pushed me beyond what I could have accomplished on my own. Together they demonstrate that real foundational support is in the authenticity of relationships built on trust.

In the process of getting to know each other, I shared the idea of the Green Bubbie with Rachel Sklar, whom I'd met at The Conversation:Jewish in America a project of The Jewish Week, that brings together Jewish movers and shakers, visionaries, educators, journalists, and philanthropists. I had been invited to the retreat in my capacity as a nationally recognized expert in Jewish early-childhood education, and Rachel as a nationally recognized social media entrepreneur. As we talked and shared—generationally apart, but with the ability to connect, to dig in and mine a conversation—Rachel started to call out to me in greeting, "Hey, Green Bubbie!" She got it, and I realized that I could be *her* Green Bubbie!

Mirele Goldsmith, another early Green Bubbie prototype, and her husband, (Green Uncle) Richard Marker, regularly open their apartment for Shabbat dinners, surrounding it with local "sprouts." They epitomize the hospitality that all Green Bubbies strive to offer. Thanks also to my friend and teacher Simi Peters. And to Miriam Healy, who insisted on the importance of sharing my ideas "out loud" with a wide array of people even beyond my own faith community. And to Gail Gundle, my very first sprout!

I am so grateful to Martha Jablow for encouraging me to just send her my notes, all of them, and confirming early on that I really did have a book in me—and a lyrical one at that! I appreciate all of her supportive editorial assistance.

Joan Betesh used her legal expertise to work through the final drafts to help me think more like a writer than a painter; her patience, clarity, and friendship are greatly appreciated.

It was my close friend Rivke Ausubel Danzig, A"H, who sparked my spiritual development. I met Rivke when I was in my early 40s. At the time, I considered myself religious. I observed holidays, I went to synagogue, I followed the rules. But, with Rivke's guidance, I began to learn that I only really knew about the practice of Judaism; I knew what we as Jews do, but not what we are capable of becoming. While I prayed at services, I didn't really appreciate the power or the practice of prayer; I didn't know that praying was something I could do at home, and on my own. With her combined doctorate in social work and her love of the Torah, she taught me what it means to be a fully developed human being. In our 18 years of friendship, until her untimely death, she shared her life of faith and prayer. Rivke taught me to appreciate what it means to have a soul, a *neshama*. She helped me recognize that the soul is a much more profound, powerful, and sustaining source for personal and interpersonal growth than either the psyche or the intellect.

During the writing of this book, I stopped all other professional endeavors. Therefore, I would like to thank the United States Social Security Administration for its ongoing financial support. It was less than I anticipated, but I am incredibly grateful it is (still) there.

In this lifetime, we are blessed if we have friends, and I feel especially blessed to have many. All of my friends that I have spoken with in the past few years have definitely contributed to the writing and completion of this book. But I must single out my best friend, Susie Kron, and not only because we've been friends for more than 50 years. I know I'm funny, but I've always been even funnier with Susie. She has great wit, wisdom, and spiritual strength. She is, and has always been, my go-to person on all things current—in politics, contemporary culture, and entertainment. She is a professional editor par excellence, and her willingness to help and her generosity of spirit has given new meaning to the term "free"lance editing, if you know what I mean!

Finally, I want to thank my husband, Rabbi Dr. Gedalia Feldman, (also known as Gary) for everything. For everything in my life has been made possible because of his love and devotion and his optimism that someday I will actually do my fair share of our life together. And heartfelt thanks to my children and their spouses for their ongoing love and their encouragement to finish the book and to "keep it short."

While the words in this book are my own, any profound ideas come from what I have learned from Torah and from the words of our Sages; any errors are my own. The timeless truths I have tried to share have been transmitted to me by all of the rabbis and teachers I have been blessed to learn with throughout my life.

Made in the USA
Charleston, SC
30 January 2014